BookFarm   9/08

D0853771

BookFarm   9/08

D-DAY

THE LIBERATION OF EUROPE BEGINS

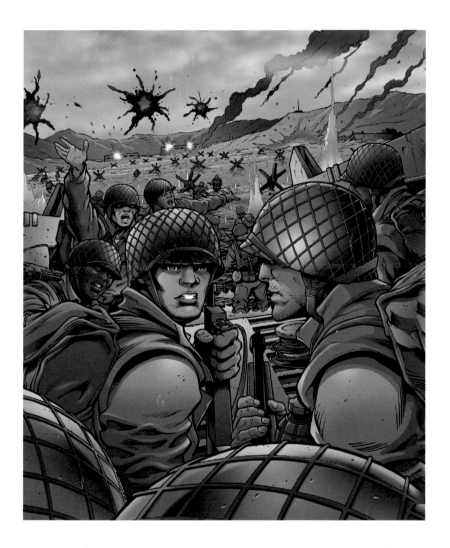

By **Doug Murray** Illustrated by **Anthony Williams**

New York

Published in 2008 by The Rosen Publishing Group, Inc.
29 East 21st Street, New York, NY 10010

Copyright © 2008 Rosen Book Works, LLC, New York, NY, and Osprey Publishing, Ltd, Oxford, England

First edition, 2008

Photo Credits:

Pp. 4, 5 (top),7 (top and bottom), 44 (inset) National Archives and Records Administration; pp. 5 (bottom), 44 courtesy of Imperial War Museums; p. 6 map created by The Map Studio; p. 45 AKG Berlin.

Library of Congress Cataloging-in-Publication Data

Murray, Doug.
  D-Day : the liberation of Europe begins / by Doug Murray ; illustrated by Anthony Williams.
  p. cm. -- (Graphic battles of World War II)
  Includes bibliographical references and index.
  ISBN-13: 978-1-4042-0786-8 (library binding)   978-1-4042-7430-3 (pbk.)
  6-pack ISBN-13: 978-1-4042-7431-0

  1. World War, 1939–1945--Campaigns--France–Normandy. 2. Normandy (France)–History. I.
Williams, Anthony. II. Title.
  D762.N6M87 2008
  940.54'21421--dc22
                                2007026859

CONTENTS

WORLD WAR II, 1939-1945

Even after World War I (1914–1919), there were strong hostilities between many nations. The United States worked to build good relations with other countries.

However, other nations were becoming aggressive toward their neighbors. In 1936, Italy invaded Ethiopia. Japan attacked China in 1937. In 1938, Germany took control of Austria and Czechoslovakia.

In 1939, Germany invaded Poland. France and England responded by declaring war on Germany. The United States had avoided fighting in the growing worldwide conflict, but on December 7, 1941, Japan attacked the U.S. naval base at Pearl Harbor, Hawaii. America was at war.

For the next four years, the United States and its allies fought Germany and the other Axis forces on land, on sea, and in the air. One of the most decisive campaigns, in 1944 was the D-day invasion, where the Allies planned to take back Europe. Its outcome was so important that many historians call this campaign the turning point of the war.

KEY COMMANDERS

General Dwight David Eisenhower
was Supreme Commander Allied Expeditionary Force. He was in charge of all Allied troops in the European theater.

General Bernard Law Montgomery
was commander of the British Eighth Army—the famous "Desert Rats" who defeated Rommel in North Africa. He was then appointed to be Eisenhower's chief deputy in planning Operation Overlord.

Field Marshal Erwin Rommel
was relieved from command of the famed "Afrika Corps" before their final defeat in North Africa and transferred to France.

Adolf Hitler
was leader of Germany and commander of German forces from 1934. Hitler began his conquering of Europe in Poland in 1939.

FIGHTING BACK

After the British Expeditionary Force had been evacuated from the European mainland in 1940, the German army had gained control of the bulk of western Europe. From that time forward, all operations against the Nazis were limited to areas away from the German homeland.

British, and later, American forces were confined to operations in North Africa and, after a seaborne assault, Crete, Sicily, and finally, mainland Italy.

In the East, the Russians were fighting against Hitler's main forces practically single-handedly.

It was clear that it would be necessary to open a second front in Europe if only to lessen the pressure on the Russians.

Planning for an invasion began as early as 1943, and after eliminating the option of going through the Balkans or continuing through Italy, it was agreed that an attack upon northern France offered the best chance of success—and the shortest route to the German homeland.

The Americans, at first, wanted to stage two amphibious assaults—one on Northwestern France, a second along the French Mediterranean. However, it was decided that there just weren't enough men and equipment to make this feasible.

They then looked at the Pas de Calais, across the narrowest point of the English Channel. It had the advantage of a good port and offered the shortest route into Germany, through the Low Countries. However, it was also the most obvious target and the one the Germans were most diligently fortifying to protect.

Next most likely was Normandy. The Bay of Seine offered some shelter from bad weather and there were enough beaches that were suitable for assault by sea. Normandy was also

The north coast of France was dotted with concrete gun fortifications. The Germans were heavily sheltered when firing the guns, such as shown here, and this proved deadly for the Allies on D-Day.

4

Senior American commanders on D-Day were (*above, left to right*) Lt. Gen Omar Bradley, Maj. Gen. Leonard Gerow, Gen. Dwight Eisenhower, and Gen. J. Lawson Collins.

less likely to be as heavily defended as Calais.

Normandy did lack large ports, but the British had already begun to develop an artificial harbor that would be enough to move men and machines until a more substantial port could be seized.

The first draft of the "Overlord" plan was completed in July 1943, and it was quickly approved by the combined Allied Chiefs of Staff. Full planning began at once.

Planning for the invasion was a massive undertaking. Every available space in England was used to store vehicles, such as these Cromwell and Churchill tanks(*above*), and the equipment needed for the attack.

The Germans were aware that an Allied invasion of France was coming. Field Marshal Erwin Rommel had been given command of the French beaches in late 1943 and, after a thorough survey, had taken action to fortify and protect all the beaches.

Meanwhile, General Eisenhower, after canceling June 5 as the invasion date, decided to move forward on June 6.

The Allied invasion now started with the deployment of airborne elements. The American 82nd and 101st Divisions along with the British 6th and 1st Canadian Parachute Regiment were sent into France on the night of July 5; their job was to secure the battlefield by blowing up bridges over rivers at enemy approach roads. Additionally, they were to hold key bridges to allow troops from the seaborne invasion force access to the mainland once they were off the beaches.

Meanwhile, the largest Allied fleet ever assembled began to disembark its troops on beaches off the coast of France. Warships began a fierce bombardment of German positions, joined by aircraft flying sortie after sortie. Despite this, German fire and preset obstacles took their toll on the

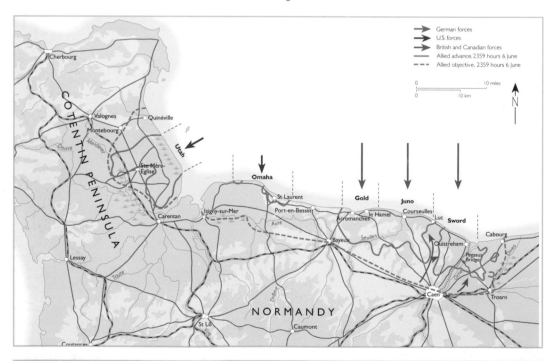

Allied forces landed on five French beaches, codenamed Utah, Omaha, Gold, Juno, and Sword. The plan was simple—defeat the Axis forces and take back Europe.

seaborne troops. Many died without ever reaching the beaches, and once ashore, many more found themselves trapped by heavy German fire.

Omaha Beach was the worst. Tank support should have been provided by DD (Dual Drive) tanks sent in along with the troops. However, most of the tanks sunk in the heavy seas and others were never launched. The American troops found themselves under heavy and continuous fire, and for a time, the attack at Omaha was in doubt. Successful reinforcements and good leadership on the beach managed to save them, and they finally made a breakthrough to higher ground.

Meanwhile, landings at Sword, Gold, Juno, and Utah beaches were successful. German opposition was light, much of it diverted toward the airborne landings. Other elements were held back by problems in the German chain of command. This lack of German attack allowed the Allies to break through the existing defenses and, by the end of the day, begin to move inland, hooking up with airborne units as they moved. A beachhead had been established, and the Allies were firmly launched in their crusade to reconquer western Europe.

The waves were choppy on the morning of the attack, and the men suffered heavily from seasickness in their landing craft.

D-DAY
THE LIBERATION OF EUROPE BEGINS

LATE SPRING, 1944. THE GERMAN ARMY IS LOSING ITS GRIP ON WESTERN EUROPE AS ALLIED ARMIES TAKE COMMAND IN NORTH AFRICA AND ITALY.

GERMAN FIELD MARSHAL ERWIN ROMMEL HAD BEEN GIVEN RESPONSIBILITY FOR THE DEFENSE OF THE ATLANTIC COAST.

HE KNOWS THAT IF GIVEN TIME HE CAN MAKE AN ALLIED INVASION DIFFICULT—PERHAPS IMPOSSIBLE.

IF GIVEN ENOUGH TIME...

THE GERMANS KNOW THAT THE ALLIES HAVE NEVER MOUNTED AN INVASION IN BAD WEATHER. AND THE WEATHER THIS JUNE HAS BEEN VERY BAD...

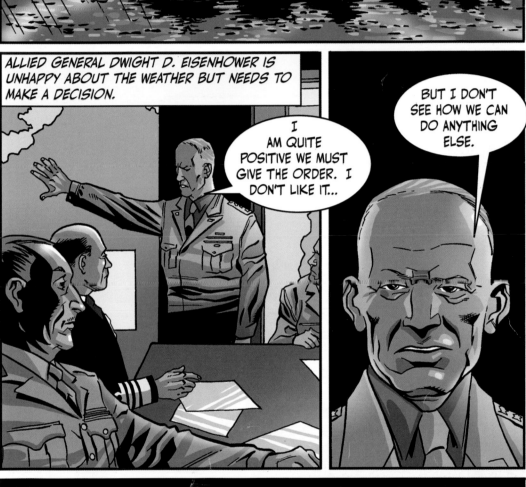

ALLIED GENERAL DWIGHT D. EISENHOWER IS UNHAPPY ABOUT THE WEATHER BUT NEEDS TO MAKE A DECISION.

I AM QUITE POSITIVE WE MUST GIVE THE ORDER. I DON'T LIKE IT...

BUT I DON'T SEE HOW WE CAN DO ANYTHING ELSE.

NIGHT. JUNE 5, 1944...

CORPORAL KERMIT LATTA, LIKE THE REST OF THE 101ST AIRBORNE, SPENDS THE NIGHT HOURS PREPARING FOR THE FLIGHT INTO OCCUPIED FRANCE.

HE HAS A NOTABLE VISITOR...

WHERE'S YOUR HOME, CORPORAL?

PENNSYLVANIA, SIR.

I BET YOU GOT THOSE SHOULDERS WORKING IN A COAL MINE! GOOD LUCK TO YOU TONIGHT, SOLDIER.

FROM WELFORD, MEMBURY, RAMSBURY, ALDERMASTON, AND ALL THE AIRFIELDS THROUGHOUT ENGLAND, THE SAME SIGHT IS REPEATED, THE SAME SOUND HEARD...

THE AIRBORNE TROOPS ARE ON THEIR WAY...

THEIR JOB IS TO SECURE BRIDGES, BLOCK ROADS, AND STOP GERMAN REINFORCEMENTS FROM REACHING THE BEACHES.

THEY ARE THE VERY TIP OF THE ALLIED SPEARHEAD.

THE FIRST ACTION IS TO BE BY A BRITISH GLIDER FORCE.

SURPRISE IS VITAL IF THEY ARE TO COMPLETE THEIR JOB.

MAJOR JOHN HOWARD WATCHES AS HIS GLIDER APPROACHES THE LANDING ZONE (LZ). HIS DIFFICULT TASK IS TO TAKE AND HOLD THE TWO BRIDGES OVER THE ORNE RIVER AND CAEN CANAL BEHIND ENEMY LINES.

HERE WE GO, MEN!

HOWARD KNOWS THAT IF THE BRIDGES CAN BE HELD, GERMAN REINFORCEMENTS WILL BE PREVENTED FROM REACHING THE CANADIAN AND BRITISH BEACH INVASIONS.

HE ALSO KNOWS HE HAS ONLY ONE COMPANY OF MEN TO DO IT WITH.

COME ON, LADS!

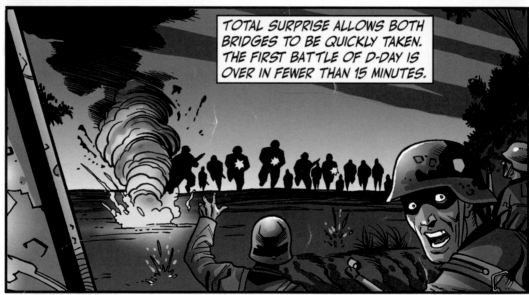

TOTAL SURPRISE ALLOWS BOTH BRIDGES TO BE QUICKLY TAKEN. THE FIRST BATTLE OF D-DAY IS OVER IN FEWER THAN 15 MINUTES.

HOWARD ORDERS HIS 180 MEN TO HOLD THE BRIDGES UNTIL THEY ARE RELIEVED.

...NO MATTER HOW LONG THAT MAY TAKE.

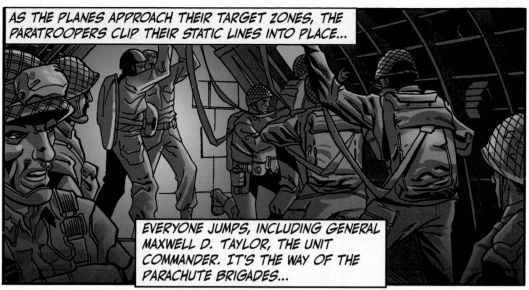

AS THE PLANES APPROACH THEIR TARGET ZONES, THE PARATROOPERS CLIP THEIR STATIC LINES INTO PLACE...

EVERYONE JUMPS, INCLUDING GENERAL MAXWELL D. TAYLOR, THE UNIT COMMANDER. IT'S THE WAY OF THE PARACHUTE BRIGADES...

THEN THE UNEXPECTED...

A BANK OF CLOUDS SUD-DENLY APPEARS OVER THE FINAL APPROACH

THE PILOTS HAVE TO ACT QUICKLY TO AVOID COLLISIONS...

OOOFH!

AAARGH!

THE UNEXPECTED CLOUDS HAVE BROKEN UP THE AIR FORMATIONS...

WE'RE THERE! GO, GO, GO!

... A FACT UNKNOWN TO THE TROOPS JUMPING INTO BATTLE.

MEN GET LOST IN THE WATER AS THEY FALL INTO FLOODED AREAS.

NORMANDY MARSH-LAND HAD BEEN FLOODED BY THE GERMANS.

UNNNFFFF!

GET MOVING, MEN!

OTHERS LAND SAFELY AND ARE QUICKLY GATHERED INTO UNITS BY THEIR OFFICERS.

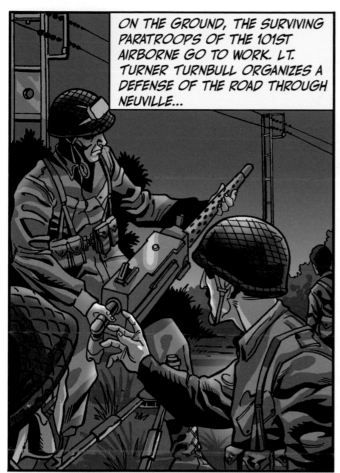

ON THE GROUND, THE SURVIVING PARATROOPS OF THE 101ST AIRBORNE GO TO WORK. LT. TURNER TURNBULL ORGANIZES A DEFENSE OF THE ROAD THROUGH NEUVILLE...

...WHILE LT. RICHARD WINTERS AND HIS MEN TAKE ON A HIDDEN BATTERY OF GERMAN CANNON.

ALL OVER THE COTENTIN PENINSULA, AIRBORNE TROOPS—OUTNUMBERED, OUTGUNNED, AND ALONE—PREPARE TO HOLD THEIR GROUND.

THE FIRST LIGHT OF DAWN OVER OMAHA BEACH...

GERMAN MAJOR WERNER PLUSKAT HAS BEEN AT HIS POST SINCE THE FIRST REPORTS OF PARACHUTE LANDINGS WERE RELAYED TO HIS HEADQUARTERS.

HE IS COLD, TIRED, AND UNSURE OF WHAT IS REALLY HAPPENING.

UNTIL...

MEIN GOTT!*

* OH MY GOD!

MAJOR PLUSKAT IS A GOOD SOLDIER, BUT IN THIS MOMENT HE KNOWS THIS IS THE END OF THE WAR FOR GERMANY.

IT IS THE INVASION! TEN THOUSAND SHIPS!

AS THE GERMANS RUSH TO THEIR DEFENSES, OFF THE SHORES OF NORMANDY...

OPEN FIRE!

THE WARSHIPS OF THE INVASION FLEET OPEN FIRE. HUNDREDS OF SHELLS SCREAM OVER THE WATER...

...HITTING PRESELECTED TARGETS ALL ALONG THE NORMANDY BEACHHEAD.

ALLIED AIRCRAFT NOW BEGIN AN ASSAULT ON THEIR TARGET: THE GERMAN GUNS TRAINED ON OMAHA BEACH.

CAPTAIN ALLEN W. STEPHENS IS FLYING HIS TWENTY-FIRST MISSION. HE IS AWED BY THE NUMBER OF SHIPS AND MEN HE SEES BELOW.

BUT ONCE OVER THE BEACH, HE AND HIS CREW CANNOT SEE THEIR TARGETS. RELUCTANTLY, THEY FLY FARTHER INLAND TO DROP THEIR BOMBS: LEAVING THE GERMAN COASTAL GUNS UNTOUCHED.

AS THE BARRAGE CONTINUES, AMERICAN TROOPS HEAD FOR UTAH AND OMAHA BEACHES.

THE BOMBARDMENT FROM THE "SEA WALL" WHISTLES OVER THEIR HEADS AS AIRCRAFT MAKE THEIR FINAL ATTACKS ON THE FRENCH MAINLAND.

THE NOISE IS DEAFENING.

STAFF SERGEANT ALFRED EIGENBERG, AN ARMY MEDIC, HAD FEARED THAT HE WOULD GET SEASICK...

BUT THE NEED TO BAIL OUT THE BOAT PUSHES EVERYTHING ELSE OUT OF HIS MIND.

SOME MEN IN OTHER LANDING CRAFT DON'T RESPOND AS QUICKLY. THEY DIE IN SIGHT OF THE BEACH—WITHOUT FIRING A SHOT.

THE 741ST TANK BATTALION IS ASSIGNED TO SUPPORT THE LANDINGS ON OMAHA BEACH.

BUT THE WATER IS ROUGHER THAN ANTICIPATED, AND THE HIGH SURF POUNDS THE TANKS AS SOON AS THEY ENTER THE WATER.

WAVES TEAR THROUGH THE TANKS' CANVAS WATER WINGS, BREAKING SUPPORT BEAMS AND FLOODING ENGINES.

THOSE TANKS SINK AND PULL THEIR CREWS DOWN UNDER THE WATER.

COMMANDERS, OUT OF CONTACT AND UNAWARE THAT THEY HAVE LOST THEIR ARMOR SUPPORT, CONTINUE WITH THE OMAHA BEACH LANDINGS...

LANDING CRAFT GET AS CLOSE TO THE BEACH AS THEY CAN—UNTIL THEY MEET THE OBSTACLES ERECTED BY THE GERMANS.

THE MEN DO WHAT THEY HAVE BEEN TRAINED TO DO. THEY MOVE FORWARD, CROUCH, AND FIRE.

UNFORTUNATELY, THERE IS NOTHING FOR THEM TO FIRE AT!

TARGETS ARE HARD TO FIND, AND IT'S A STRUGGLE TO STAY UPRIGHT.

DESPERATE SOLDIERS ABANDON THEIR EQUIPMENT AS THEY TRY TO REACH THE BEACH.

SGT. TOM VALENCE, A RIFLE SERGEANT IN A-COMPANY OF THE 116TH INFANTRY, IS HIT IN THE HAND AS HE LEAVES HIS BOAT.

HE TRIES TO SHOOT BACK BUT HIS RIFLE WILL NOT WORK.

SGT. VALENCE KEEPS MOVING FORWARD...

HE KNOWS IT IS IMPOSSIBLE TO KNOCK OUT A GERMAN CONCRETE EMPLACEMENT WITH A .30-CALIBER RIFLE—BUT HE IS DETERMINED TO FIGHT.

HE IS HIT AGAIN, AND AGAIN...

WOUNDED AND EXHAUSTED, VALENCE FINALLY FINDS SHELTER—ONE LIVE BODY AMONG MANY DEAD ONES.

THE STORY IS THE SAME ALONG THE LENGTH OF OMAHA BEACH...

23

THE DROPPING OF RAMPS SEEMS A SIGNAL FOR CONCENTRATED AND MURDEROUS GERMAN MACHINE-GUN FIRE.

ALL ALONG THE LENGTH OF OMAHA BEACH, OTHER ALLIED TROOPS LIE, IN THE HUNDREDS, HUDDLED BEHIND WHAT COVER THEY CAN FIND...

...AND WAIT.

AS THE AMERICANS LIE PINNED DOWN BY THE SEVERE FIRE ON OMAHA BEACH, THE CANADIAN DIVISION BEGINS ITS ASSAULT ON JUNO BEACH.

ROUGH SEAS HAVE DELAYED THE CANADIANS' LANDINGS. HIGH TIDE HID THE GERMAN TRAPS AWAITING THE INVADERS OF THE NORMANDY COAST...

...MINES, CONTACT-FUSED SHELLS, AND ALL MANNER OF DEATH TRAPS.

...TRAPS THAT CANNOT BE AVOIDED.

COME ON, MEN!

BUT EVEN WHEN THEIR LANDING CRAFT ARE DAMAGED OR SUNK, MOST OF THE INFANTRY IS ABLE TO STRUGGLE ASHORE.

AND UNLIKE OMAHA BEACH, THEIR ARMOR SUPPORT ARRIVED VERY QUICKLY.

WITH GREAT COURAGE AND DISCIPLINE THE CANADIANS BEGIN THEIR ASSAULT.

THE GERMANS PREPARE THEIR OWN FIRE, KNOWING THEY HAVE ONLY A FEW MINUTES TO BLUNT THE LANDING OR BE KILLED.

THE REGINA RIFLE REGIMENT HAS BEEN ASSIGNED TO TAKE THE VILLAGE OF COURSEULLES, THE STRONGEST POINT IN THE AREA. THE VILLAGE AND ITS HARBOR HAVE BEEN DIVIDED INTO 12 SECTORS, EACH TO BE TAKEN BY ONE PLATOON.

"A" COMPANY LANDED DIRECTLY UNDER THE GUNS OF THE GERMAN DEFENDERS. THEY IMMEDIATELY BEGIN TO MOVE TO SUPPRESS THE FIRE.

MOVE IT, MEN!

AAARRGGH!

THEY ARE COVERED BY THE TANKS OF THE 1ST HUSSARS.

THE MEN OF CANADA'S QUEEN'S OWN RIFLES, LED BY LT. W. G. HERBERT, HAVE A MUCH HARDER TIME. TIDE AND WIND HAVE TAKEN THEM 200 YARDS EAST OF THEIR PLANNED LANDING—AND RIGHT INTO THE FIRE OF THE GERMAN GUNS IN THE VILLAGE OF BERNIÈRES.

TRAPPED UNDER HEAVY FIRE, MAN AFTER MAN DROPS INTO THE BOILING SURF.

LT. HERBERT KNOWS THAT SOMETHING HAS TO BE DONE QUICKLY OR THE BEACHHEAD WILL BE LOST.

HE, LANCE CORPORAL RENÉ TESSIER AND RIFLEMAN WILL CHICOSKI BREAK FOR THE SEA WALL...

ONCE THERE, THEY ARE ABLE TO USE ITS TEN-FOOT HEIGHT FOR COVER AS THEY INCH TOWARD THE GERMAN STRONGPOINT...

THEY ARE ABLE TO DESTROY THE GERMANS INSIDE.

FOR THEIR ACTION, ALL THREE MEN ARE AWARDED THE LEGION OF MERIT* AND THE MILITARY CROSS.

*THE LEGION OF MERIT IS AWARDED TO CANADIAN ARMED FORCES FOR EXCEPTIONAL MILITARY ACTIONS.

THE ACTIONS OF THESE MEN AND OTHERS LIKE THEM HELP MOST OF THE TWO LEADING REGIMENTS SAFELY ASHORE AND READY TO MOVE INLAND.

THE GERMANS HAD LAID ABOUT 14,000 MINES BETWEEN COURSEULLES AND BERNIÈRES. BUT ALLIED ENGINEERS WORK TO CLEAR THE WAY, MAKING GAPS TO HELP TROOPS BEGIN TO MOVE INLAND...

...OFF THE BEACH, AND INTO FRANCE.

AT GOLD BEACH, THE BRITISH BEGIN THEIR OWN ATTACK.

GERMAN FIRE IS HEAVY, BUT NOTHING LIKE THAT ON OMAHA BEACH. BRITISH TROOPS QUICKLY GET OFF THE BEACH AND ONTO HIGHER GROUND.

SEEING HIS MEN PINNED DOWN BY MACHINE-GUN FIRE, SGT. MAJOR HOLLIS OF THE GREEN HOWARDS LAUNCHES AN IMMEDIATE ASSAULT.

HOLLIS HATES THE GERMANS. AT DUNKIRK,* HE HAD SEEN THE BODIES OF FRENCH MEN, WOMEN, AND CHILDREN KILLED BY THE NAZIS.

*DUNKIRK IS A FRENCH CITY THAT WAS THE SITE OF HEAVY FIGHTING IN 1940.

EVER SINCE, HE HAD BECOME A HUNTER OF THE ENEMY.

WITHIN MINUTES, HE DESTROYS THE PILLBOX, KILLING THE TWO GERMAN SOLDIERS WHO WERE OPERATING THE MACHINE GUN.

SOON AFTER, HE IS INSTRUMENTAL IN THE CAPTURE OF A LARGE NUMBER OF GERMAN SOLDIERS WHO ARE SUPPORTING THE MACHINE GUNS.

LATER THAT DAY, HOLLIS ATTACKS A GERMAN FIELD GUN AND SAVES TWO MEN TRAPPED BY ITS FIRE. HE WAS AWARDED THE VICTORIA CROSS–THE ONLY WINNER OF THAT DECORATION ON D-DAY.

AT LA RIVIÈRE, THE EAST YORKSHIRE DIVISION IS UNDER HEAVY FIRE. THEY HAVE CALLED FOR NAVAL SUPPORT.

HEAVY SHELLING FORCES THE GERMANS TO DUCK FOR COVER.

THE 88MM WEAPON WAS SOON SILENCED AND 40 GERMAN PRISONERS ARE TAKEN.

IT TAKES SEVERAL HOURS OF HOUSE-TO-HOUSE FIGHTING TO CLEAR THE VILLAGE, BUT IN THAT TIME THE ENTIRE AREA IS TAKEN, ALLOWING THE BRITISH COLUMN TO ADVANCE TOWARD VER SUR MER.

GOLD BEACH WAS SECURE.

31

LT. COLONEL JAMES RUDDER'S THREE RANGER COMPANIES HAVE BEEN ORDERED TO DESTROY THE LARGE COASTAL ARTILLERY CANNONS BETWEEN OMAHA AND UTAH BEACHES THAT MENACE THE AMERICAN BEACHES ON EITHER SIDE.

BUT DELAYED BY A NAVIGATION ERROR, THEY ARE LATE—AND THE GERMANS ARE READY FOR THEM.

SOME MEN DO NOT WAIT FOR THE ROPES AND BEGIN CLIMBING BY HAND.

OTHERS, LIKE PRIVATE FIRST CLASS (PFC) HARRY ROBERTS, HAVE ALREADY HAD ROPES CUT TWO AND THREE TIMES.

SGT. BILL PETTY, ON HIS WAY UP FOR THE THIRD TIME, WATCHES AS A SOLDIER TO HIS RIGHT IS HIT BY GERMAN GUNFIRE.

DESPERATE, PETTY AND HIS COMRADES REACH THE TOP...

SCRAMBLING FOR COVER FROM THE GERMAN FIRE...

ONCE OVER THE EDGE OF THE CLIFF, THE RANGERS ARE ABLE TO FINISH THE LAST GERMAN DEFENDERS.

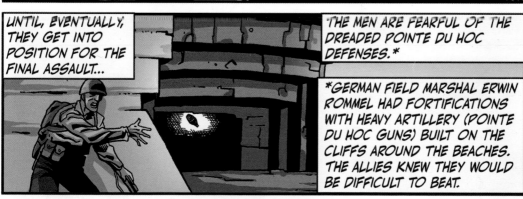

TRAINING COMES INTO PLAY AS SGT. PETTY, PFC ROBERTS, AND OTHER SURVIVING RANGERS MOVE FORWARD TOWARD THEIR TARGET.

UNTIL, EVENTUALLY, THEY GET INTO POSITION FOR THE FINAL ASSAULT...

THE MEN ARE FEARFUL OF THE DREADED POINTE DU HOC DEFENSES.*

*GERMAN FIELD MARSHAL ERWIN ROMMEL HAD FORTIFICATIONS WITH HEAVY ARTILLERY (POINTE DU HOC GUNS) BUILT ON THE CLIFFS AROUND THE BEACHES. THE ALLIES KNEW THEY WOULD BE DIFFICULT TO BEAT.

SGT. PETTY AND HIS MEN ARRIVE AT THE BUNKERS. THEY FIND NO GUNS.

TWO HOURS LATER A PATROL FINDS FIVE BIG GUNS AND AMMUNITION A FEW MILES AWAY, THE POINTE DU HOC GUNS.

AS TROOPS MOVE INLAND FROM UTAH, SWORD, GOLD, AND JUNO BEACHES, THOSE AT OMAHA ARE STILL PINNED DOWN. THEY ARE CAUGHT BETWEEN THE SEA AND THE HEAVY FIRE OF THE GERMAN DEFENDERS.

THINGS ARE SO BAD THAT AMERICAN GENERAL OMAR BRADLEY IS THINKING ABOUT GIVING UP AND PULLING THE TROOPS BACK FROM OMAHA BEACH.

BUT GENERAL NORMAN COTA IS NOT READY TO GIVE UP...

STRIDING THROUGH THE RAIN OF FIRE, HE ORDERS A GROUP OF RANGERS TO LEAD THE WAY OFF THE BEACH...

COTA LEADS BY EXAMPLE—AND THE MEN OF OMAHA BEACH BEGIN TO FOLLOW HIM.

NOT FAR AWAY, A SECOND LEADER STEPS FORWARD. COLONEL CHARLES D. CANHAM, COMMANDER OF THE 116TH.

THEY'RE MURDERING US HERE!

LET'S MOVE INLAND AND GET MURDERED!

MEN LOSE THEIR FEAR AS THEIR LEADERS TAKE COMMAND OF THE SITUATION.

ONCE MOVING, THEY DO NOT STOP.

AS THEY MOVE, THE SECOND AND THIRD WAVES OF LANDING TROOPS COME IN. THE BOTTLE-NECK ON THE BEACH IS FINALLY BROKEN.

AS THE ALLIED FORCES BEGIN TO MAKE THEIR WAY OFF THE BEACHES, THE GERMANS FINALLY BEGIN TO REACT. GENERAL ERICH MARCKS KNOWS THAT IF THE BRITISH CAPTURED CAEN, ALL WOULD BE LOST...

IF YOU DON'T SUCCEED IN THROWING THE BRITISH BACK INTO THE SEA, WE SHALL HAVE LOST THE WAR!

"I HAVE TWO BATTALIONS, SIR. I WILL DO WHAT I CAN!"

MOST GERMAN TANKS INSIDE FRANCE WERE UNDER THE DIRECT COMMAND OF ADOLF HITLER'S HEADQUARTERS. ONLY A VERY FEW WERE AVAILABLE FOR THE DEFENSE OF NORMANDY.

THOSE FEW BEGAN TO ROLL TOWARD THE BEACHES.

UNFORTUNATELY FOR THE GERMANS, THE 2ND BATTALION KINGS SHROPSHIRE LIGHT INFANTRY HAD BEEN ALERTED TO THEIR MOVEMENTS.

HURRY UP! LINE UP RIGHT HERE! THEY'LL HAVE TO COME THROUGH US TO REACH THE BEACHES!

AS PREDICTED, THE GERMAN FORCE CAME STRAIGHT AT THE CAREFULLY PLACED ANTITANK WEAPONS.

OPEN FIRE!

THE GERMAN ARMOR WAS MET BY A HAIL OF FIRE.

FOUR TANKS WERE IMMEDIATELY KNOCKED OUT.

THE OTHERS VEERED TO THE LEFT...

...WHERE THEY MET THE STAFFORDSHIRE YEOMANRY'S 17-POUND GUNS.

THE ADVANCE IS STOPPED BEFORE IT CAN REACH THE MEN ON THE BEACHES.

BACK AT THE KEY BRIDGES OVER THE CAEN RIVER, MAJOR HOWARD CONTINUES TO HOLD.

BUT HIS RESOURCES ARE RUNNING THIN AND HIS MEN GROWING TIRED.

I THINK I HEAR BAGPIPES!

YOU'RE DAFT!

NO! LOOK! THEY'RE HERE!

IT IS THE FIRST OF MANY LINKUPS BETWEEN THE AIRBORNE TROOPS AND THEIR COMRADES FROM THE BEACHES...

...AN INDICATION THAT THE INVASION HAS SUCCEEDED!

AS NIGHT FALLS ON OMAHA BEACH, GENERAL NORMAN COTA GAZES AT THE SURF.

HE FINDS HIMSELF VERY TIRED.

BUT THERE IS NO TIME FOR REST NOW.

RUN ME UP THE HILL, SON.

AS GENERAL COTA REJOINS HIS TROOPS, STAFF SGT. ALFRED EIGENBERG, MEDIC, TAKES A BREAK.

HE HAS LOST COUNT OF THE NUMBER OF WOUNDED HE HAS TREATED SINCE HIS LEAKING BOAT MADE IT TO SHORE.

HE IS BONE TIRED—BUT THERE IS ONE THING HE MUST DO BEFORE HE SLEEPS...

Dear Mom and Dad.

By now you've heard of the invasion...

Well, I'm all right...

THE END

THE BEGINING OF THE END

The invasion of Normandy and the opening of a second front in Europe was the greatest disaster Hitler and the German army had ever received. Aside from the presence of attacking Allied forces in Europe, it also cut the Germans off from the French Atlantic ports. This also meant an end to the German U-boat war in the Atlantic.

Worse, the loss of the French coast deprived the Luftwaffe of its early-warning radar systems, allowing Allied bombers easier access to the German cities. Later, as French airfields were captured, it also meant full-time Allied fighter bombings and support for their troops.

As the Allies advanced through France, the Russians broke through more enemy lines and began a succession of attacks into the eastern flank of the German Reich.

German industry, bombed by the

Once the Allies captured French airfields, they began full-time bombings of German troops across France and Germany. This destruction of resources helped lead to the end for Germany.
(inset) German infantrymen captured by the Allies on D-Day were taken to prisoner-of-war camps in England. Most were between eighteen and ninteen years old.

The final collapse of Germany happened once American and Soviet forces met each other in central Germany on April 21 1945.

Allies and denied resources by the loss of key areas, began to falter. France had provided more than half the food needed by the German armies; this was soon lost. The loss of other French resources meant that needed weapons and equipment were not delivered quickly enough to the frontline units.

The German army began to retreat, contracting their defensive lines until they stood on the banks of the Rhine itself. By early 1945, Allied bombers were smashing through the German railway system, cutting off food and supplies to the interior of the country. Soon after, the Allied armies moved into German territory both from the east and the west. By April 25, Russian and American troops had met in several parts of Germany. The war was lost, and on April 30, Adolf Hitler committed suicide.

It had taken just eleven months from the first moment the first Allied troops touched the ground in occupied France until Germany surrendered. The war in Europe was over.

allies People or countries that give support to each other.

amphibious Coordinated land, sea, and air forces organized for invasion.

artillery Large guns that are mounted.

assault A military attack that involves direct fighting.

bail To remove water from a boat by using a container to dip and throw the water overboard.

battalion A large group of military troops.

bombardment An attack that is done with heavy gunfire.

deployment To extend a military unit, especially in width.

diligent Steady, energetic effort.

emplacement A place that has been prepared by the military for weapons.

foothold Position usable as a base for further advance.

fortification A building created to defend or strengthen a place or position.

glider An aircraft similar to an airplane but without an engine.

hostilities Conflict between two parties which usually leads to warfare.

Hussars Members of European armies that copied the Hungarian cavalry of the fifteenth century.

infantry The branch of an army trained to fight on foot.

instrumental Being a vital part of getting something done.

invasion The act of sending armed forces to another country in order to take it over.

liberation The act of setting someone free.

mainland The largest land mass of a country or continent relative to surrounding islands.

marshland An area of wetlands or marshes.

medic A person trained to give emergency medical help.

meterology A science that deals with the atmosphere and especially with weather and weather forecasting

paratrooper A member of troops that are trained to jump from an airplane.

reinforce To strengthen or support by additional assistance.

shelling Attacking with artillery.

spearhead The leading force in getting something done.

suppress To stop something from happening.

ORGANIZATIONS

Eldred World War II Museum
201 Main Street
P.O. Box 273
Eldred, PA 16731
(814) 225-2220
Web site: http://www.eldredwwiimuseum.org

The National World War II Museum
945 Magazine Street
New Orleans, LA 70130
(504) 527 6012
Web site: http://www.ddaymuseum.org

FOR FURTHER READING

Ambrose, Stephen E. *D-Day: June 6, 1944: The Climactic Battle of World War II*. New York: Simon & Schuster, 1995.
Balkoski, Joseph. *Omaha Beach: D-Day, June 6, 1944*. Mechanicsburg, PA: Stackpole Books, 2006.
Bliven, Bruce. *Invasion: The Story of D-Day*. New York: Sterling Point Books, 2007.
Bowman, Martin. *Remembering D-Day: Personal Histories of Everyday Heroes*. London: HarperCollins, 2004
Bryan Perrett. *D-Day (My Story)*. New York: Scholastic, 2004
Drez, Ronald J. *Remember D-Day: Both Sides Tell Their Stories*. Washington, DC: National Geographic Childrens Books, 2004.
Giangreco, D. M., and Kathryn Moore. *Eyewitness D-Day: Firsthand Accounts from the Landing at Normandy to the Liberation of Paris*. New York: Sterling Publishing, 2004.
Hynson, Colin. *D-Day (Days That Changed the World)*. Chicago: World Almanac Library, 2004.
Parry, Dan. *D-Day: The Dramatic Story of the World's Greatest Invasion*. London:BBC Books, 2004.
Richard Holmes. *The D-Day Experience: From Invasion to the Liberation of Paris*. London: Carlton Books, 2004

INDEX

B
Bernières, France, 28, 29
Bradley, Omar, 34
bridges, 6, 10, 11, 12, 40

C
Caen Canal/River, 11, 37, 40
Canada/Canadian troops, 6, 11, 25–27, 28–29
Canham, Charles D., 36
Chicoski, Will, 28–29
Cota, Norman, 34–35, 42–43
Courseulles, France, 27, 29

D
D-Day, launch/planning of, 4–5, 6–7
Dunkirk, France, 30

E
Eigenberg, Alfred, 19, 43
Eisenhower, Dwight D., 3, 6, 9
England/British forces, 3, 4, 5, 10, 11–12,
    30–31, 37, 38–39

F
France, as site of D-Day invasion, 4–5, 6

G
Germany/German army
invasion/control of mainland Europe, 3, 4
loses war/surrenders, 44–45
glider forces, 11–12
Gold Beach, 7, 30–31, 34

H
Herbert, W. G., 28–29
Hitler, Adolf, 3, 4, 37, 44, 45
Hollis, Major, 30
Howard, John, 11, 12, 40
Hussars, 27

J
Juno Beach, 7, 25–26, 34

L
La Rivière, France, 31
Latta, Kermit, 10

M
Marcks, Erich, 37
Montgomery, Bernard Law, 3

N
Neuville, France, 15

O
Omaha Beach, 7, 16, 18, 19, 20–25, 26, 30,
    32, 34–36, 42–43

P
parachute brigades, 6, 13–15, 16
Petty, Bill, 32–33
Pluskat, Werner, 16–17
Pointe du Hoc defenses, 33

R
Ranger companies, 32–33
Roberts, Harry, 32–33
Rommel, Erwin, 3, 6, 8, 33, 41
Russian troops, 4, 44, 45

S
Stephens, Allen W., 18
Sword Beach, 7, 34

T
Taylor, Maxwell D., 13
Tessier, René, 28–29
Turnbull, Turner, 15

U
United States/American forces, 3, 4, 19, 32, 45
Utah Beach, 7, 19, 32, 34

V
Valence, Tom, 22–23

WEB SITES

Due to the changing nature of Internet links, the Rosen Publishing Group, Inc. has developed an online list of Web sites related to the subject of this book. This site is updated regularly. Please use this link to access the list:

http://www.rosenlinks.com/gbwwt/dday